John Boyd Thacher

Charlecote - Or the Trial of William Shakespeare

John Boyd Thacher

Charlecote - Or the Trial of William Shakespeare

ISBN/EAN: 9783337058319

Printed in Europe, USA, Canada, Australia, Japan

Cover: Foto ©Thomas Meinert / pixelio.de

More available books at **www.hansebooks.com**

CHARLECOTE

OR

THE TRIAL OF WILLIAM SHAKESPEARE

BY

JOHN BOYD THACHER

ILLUSTRATED BY

CHARLES LOUIS HINTON

DODD, MEAD & COMPANY, NEW YORK
ANNO DOMINI ONE THOUSAND EIGHT
HUNDRED AND NINETY-FIVE

THIS LITTLE BOOK IS DEDICATED

TO

WILLARD FISKE

WHO TO-DAY HOLDETH THE LANDOR VILLA,

ON THE HILLSIDE OF

FIESOLE,

AND WHO FROM THE HANDS OF DISCERNING

FORTUNE HATH HAD NOT ONLY

THE FIGS AND OLIVES

BUT

THE WIT AND FANCY

OF

WALTER SAVAGE LANDOR

I

PREFACE

PREFACE

WE are in a strait to frame an excuse for what may seem to some an act of literary vandalism. When Walter Savage Landor wrote his "Citation of William Shakespeare," he gave to English literature one of its masterpieces. Whoso addeth to or taketh away from such a work committeth a literary sin. The State protects its citizen who conceives a fancy and develops it to a practical invention. Under certain conditions the State permits another to utilize the prior invention when a combination in which it is used is marked and differing. We can only creep under this protecting wing and justify ourselves in its latitude.

We have appropriated the conceit of Landor that in his early youth Shakespeare was cited before Sir Thomas Lucy, charged with the killing of a deer in the Knight's forest. We have taken his *dramatis personæ* and added to the company the figure of Hannah Hathaway. We have in a few instances employed the very words found in his work. We have run the Landorian thread in and out of our own poor loom and if the product be unsatisfactory it is because of the imperfection of our mechanical contrivances and the infelicity of the workman. But here endeth our offending. The very richness of the poet's fancy, the elegance of his diction, the loftiness of his style, the constant presence of his personality, all are gifts which belong to Landor alone and which we can neither ape nor wear.

When the Baconian theory of the authorship of Shakespeare's plays was first suggested it found some acceptance because of the unsubstantial support on which rested the personality of Shakespeare. Information concerning his life is meagre and incomplete. Cloud and shadow hide from us his presence. Where men hear a voice and behold no figure they yield to uncertain fears and doubt gets hold on them. Could a man speak as he spake, utter such thoughts, so unfold nature's secrets, so unriddle the human heart, unless that man had been **part** of the lives of a multitude of his kind ? Could such a man have walked abroad **without** touching hundreds of other real men in his London life ? **Must not such a man** have **written** countless **letters** ? Must **he not have somewhere** registered his share in **passing** events ? Yet **we** know less of this man than **of** any other literary character of **his** age. **We do** not know how he lived **nor with** whom he lived. **We** do not **know** how he **looked in form** and in feature. **His** mighty brain must have dwelt behind a high forehead and so men have drawn for us the Droeshout portrait. We do not know in what he was like unto other men, nor in what he was differing from other men. We have no specimen of his handwriting, unless it be found among five disputed signatures.

Tradition has not been bold enough to tread further on a way in which fact dare not venture. As there are scarcely three authentic facts connected with his career—beyond the record of his christening, his purchase of property and his death—so have there come down to us only about three traditions. He perhaps killed a deer in Charlecote forest. He perhaps held the horse of some courtier before the door of a play-house. He perhaps had a drinking bout with Ben Jonson in some country tavern. And this is all—all of fact and all of tradition ! History may have thought the elements of his soul too great to suffer the relation of their union with the common existence of the body, and so have swept from the record the doings of his life.

To us Shakespeare is a real man who once lived in a real world.

Landor has taken one of these few traditions and treated it as a fact. He has thus become a historian and no historian may have exclusive use of a fact. We have accepted this story of the slain deer and of Shakespeare's trial before Sir Thomas Lucy. If we acknowl-edge that the tale we here tell was first made by Landor, we may justly expect Landor to account for discrepancies and apparent inaccuracies. If there was no law against deer stealing punishable with death in the reign of Queen Elizabeth, the indictment was drawn by Landor and the degree of the crime was fixed by him.

We here try to represent Shakespeare, the youth, in three characteristic poses. In the first scene we present him as the lover, tender of affection and true in constancy. We take more than a lustrum from the years of Hannah Hathaway, that the fire of a more ardent look may be in her eye as she turns her face loveward. If she is shrewish, neither Shakespeare nor we shall guess it.

Arms of love were never made so strong that they could hold a soul like his in Stratford town, and we hear Shakespeare revealing to Hannah the challenge his spirit hath had from the outer world and for a larger life. In the second scene we present Shakespeare as the village ne'er-do-well, exchanging badinage with the yokels in the forest. He mocks but obeys the authority they magnify. In the third scene we have repainted Landor's setting of the trial, and present the youth in the consciousness of his mental supremacy, playing with the will and purposes of the Judge as deftly as Hamlet fingered the stops of his flute. If his departure through the open window is sudden and unordered, there is no resentment in his glance against the Knight, fond and foolish, but only unutterable love for his Hannah, fair and faithful.

In all this we have seen Shakespeare as a man, moving as a man, feeling as a man, speaking as a man. Shakespeare the mature poet, no pen dare familiarly describe. Shakespeare the youth, moved by ambitious thoughts and sustained by plighted love, we have even dared to approach. If the reader shall withhold from us all acknowledgment of originality, let him at least at our instance turn again to Landor's work and refresh himself with his inimitable fancy.

J. B. T.

Albany, November 5, 1895.

CHARACTERS

CHARACTERS

SIR THOMAS LUCY, Knight, Justice of the Peace

SILAS GOUGH, Chaplain

WILLIAM SHAKESPEARE, Prisoner

JOSEPH CARNABY, ⎱ Foresters, Constables and
EUSEBY TREEN, ⎰   Witnesses

HANNAH HATHAWAY

EPHRAIM BARNETT, Clerk to Sir Thomas Lucy

TIME

THE YEAR OF OUR LORD, 1582

SYNOPSIS

SCENE I.   In Front of the Cottage of Hannah
Hathaway

SCENE II.   The Park at Charlecote

SCENE III.   The Great Hall at Charlecote House

SCENE I

SCENE I

(In front of the cottage of Hannah Hatha-way. It is early evening. The cottage is in the right middle distance. As the curtain rises Silas Gough is driven out of the cottage by Hannah Hathaway with loud and vehement scoldings.)

Hannah
Hathaway

OUT, out, out, thou unholy holy-man, thou divine obstructor of righteousness, thou ecclesiastical villain, thou enemy of good, thou beguiler of thy mother's sex, thou pros-ecuting persecutor of innocent maidens !

Silas Gough

As to innocency, I am not now summoning thee before any bar and as to thy maidenly loud-crying virtues, I am not at this moment an echoing wall, but this, dear Mistress Hannah, I fain would aver and by my dress which speaks of religion, no matter what tongue I ply within my teeth, by this dress I swear, I never yet did touch a hand like that ; and well I know thy hand is no maiden's hand, but the hurler of a lusty dame's indignation and so I shall say and ever so shall I think until the blood go on coursing again from its suffused tenting in the hollow of my cheek.

Hannah
Hathaway

Thou oughtest rather to rejoice and be pricked with a timely hope of salvation at the visitation of blood to thy sin-seamed face. If blood can reach thy cheek, the power of God may yet reach thy heart. But as touching thy oath, it is false like the practice of thine own preached word and thou art forsworn. If I had but yielded this hand to thy sly but constant search each time thy presence fouled the air Heaven sent my lungs, I had now no hand, no flesh, no fingers.

Silas Gough

Oh ! Mistress Hannah, the soothing hand of the Church— (reaches out for her hand)

Hannah Hathaway

Unhand me, hand of Church ! The soothing hand

of the Church is a balm-bearing hand and the inverted palm holds it as a blessed chalice ; but thy hand is the hand of vice, thy hooked fingers clutch with unlawful seekings, thy flesh tingles with hot and vibrating desire. Thou knowest no seemliness withal. Didst thou not at the funeral rites to good Dame Mowbry but three days laid to rest, grasp my farewelling hand as I did uncurtain the death sheet from off her fastened face ?

Silas Gough

'Twas a churchly office I would have done and saved thine unfamiliar hand.

Hannah
Hathaway

How many days have gone

since at Judith Hemming's wedding thou didst seize my hand as I laid upon her head her wreath of orange promises and when, but for my caught-up care, a luckless omen had wreathed us all in pain ?

Silas Gough

It was not the cap of or-ange blossoms I did think up-on, but of thy kisses ripened for faithful wooer like the Knight's holy Chaplain and yet which thou wouldst have thrown uncounted and un-noticed on Judith's wealthy mouth.

Hannah Hathaway

Go thou and woo some toothless dame.

Silas Gough

'Tis my sweet will to woo

thine unmelting will. (Runs toward her.)

Hannah Hathaway

'Tis my sweet will that no wooer among men shall have his sweet will of me save only and forever mine own Sweet Will.

Silas Gough

Thine own Sweet Will will I some near-by day hang and I do tell thee the gibbet is already timbered and the joints eager for their firm establishment on which shall swing his bold and worthless carcass.

Hannah Hathaway

Out, out and away, I say, thou miserable exuding slime from the bottomless pit, thou rank and vegetable-grown soul, thou diseased Preacher, thou

crawling scavenger, thou creep-
ing mal-spoken thing, out,
out——

(Enter Will Shakespeare
with a gun upon his shoulder
and gazing coolly at the angry
pair, pretending not to see Si-
las.)

Will Shakespeare

How now, Hannah mine,
why so hot, when the evening
is so cool ?

Hannah Hathaway

Oh ! how to tell thee ! a
thousand plagues——

Will Shakespeare

What then hath disturbed
thee so ? It cannot have been
the temperate trees, for they
have turned their leaves face
downward for the night. It

cannot have been the birds, for they have long since tucked their pecking-tired heads beneath their mattressed wing. The village life hath stopped and no one but our two poor human selves——

Hannah Hathaway

And dost thou not see this impious priest ?

Will Shakespeare

Why, behold Master Silas, the anointed preacher to souls and parish lamp to natural feet ! But still, I do maintain I was right, for I do not think we can call *him* human, dost thou, Hannah ? Are his works manly or unmanly ? When hast thou in thy charitableness known him to do aught of

NO, NO, SILAS, THOU ART NO DOG."

manly deed or when hast thou
heard him speak a single man-
like thought? Verily, as I am
an oathable man, thou art no
human man but a thing, a
black, unpleasing, misguided,
unredeemable thing! A thing
with eyes that roll and go
backward and forward on their
axised sockets ; a thing with
ears to drink in scandal and
tattled gossip and a soul like a
trough to dough it in and knead
it into current report until the
entire parish hath fed on thine
unwholesome bread. No, thou
art no man, thou art a——

Silas Gough

Dog——

Will Shakespeare

No, no, Silas, thou art no
dog. A dog is faithful, a dog

is honest, a dog is conscionable, a dog is of good report. I would not have thee a dog, Silas, for I ever was friend of dogs.

Silas Gough

I will have thee hanged, I will have thy heart upon a stick, I will hire a brave lad to wave thy head upon a pike.

Hannah Hathaway

His mind is ever on a hanging. He hath been reading of the Apostles and of the end of his betters.

Will Shakespeare

No, no, Silas, I shall never be hanged by thee, but this I promise, I shall gibbet thee on a printed scaffold and there shalt thou swing so long as letters have a home in language, and while words exist men shall cry out as they pass thee by, " behold Silas Gough, the dreadful thing."

Silas Gough

I will run and seek Sir Thomas. Thou shalt no longer disgrace this parish or I will recite mass in the lowest hell. (Runs off.)

Will Shakespeare

What a relief the demise of his presence doth afford. Hannah, was there ever a chaplain before Heaven's gate like unto this Silas and was there ever a name like unto Gough ? Its very sound is like the departure of the imprisoned air from off the stomach and the lungs. Gough and cough and off—so lets no more of him. (Lays down his gun.)

Hannah Hathaway

Willie, Willie, he hath seen thy gun !

Will Shakespeare

What matters it? Did not the gun choke its strong desire to converse with Master Silas? It did itch and beat against mine arm as if its load must find a quick escape. It is a good, a palpable Christian gun, not fit for the base medium of uttering speech to such as Silas Gough, even if it be a gun of thine own dear sex, Hannah, and have the last of all the words. It shall have better and more wholesome food this night.

Hannah Hathaway

Art thou turning outlaw,

Will? Art thou bent on ever teasing the constables ?

Will
Shakespeare

Nay, but there is one brave deer in Charlecote forest, a haughty, blustering, a well-antler-multiplied buck, heavy with the weight of fat, into whose tantalizing eyes I have twice looked but both times have I been gunless and un-knifed. He hath challenged me to an honorable contest— *his senses*, sharper than weapons of offense and sounder than thrice protected buckler, *against my skill* with the imprisoned powder and the brutal slug. Three times have I sought him with my gun but never yet have nearer come than to see the waving defiance of his well flagged tail or to hear the whistling music of his nostril and the disdainful march of his firm and fearless tread. But I do know the way he walketh to the pool for his refreshing drink and this night shall fat Master Buck lower his flag to me.

Hannah Hathaway

But to kill the lord's deer! It is greatly punishable.

Will Shakespeare

It shall be my last deer and my last offense. Hannah, listen! When I came into the world there came with me two souls, twin in birth but twain in kind, differing in complexion and bequeathment of gifts as the lime-licked water differs from the blood of the vine. The one is my Stratford soul, the soul that lets me seek game from out the forest and at the tavern and in the vestry, that invites me to perplex magistrates and to trouble authority. My other soul is my better part, broad like the continents that drink of the waters, deep like the seas that eat of the land, high like the heavens that sup on the hope of mortals. It calls me ever by name and I listen to it as to a familiar.

Hannah
Hathaway

And with what soul lovest thou me, Will ?

Will
Shakespeare

My Stratford soul were too

Charlecote, or

mean, too common, too clayey
a thing to love thee with, my
Hannah. It is walled 'round
with very brief powers and it
tires with the exercise of mo-
ments. I would love thee with
that other soul which knows
neither bounds, nor wearyings
nor ending of days. No regis-
ter hath yet been tabled to
measure my love for thee.
The greater circle this better
soul of mine enlarges, the
greater scope shalt thou have
of my love.

Hannah
Hathaway

But whither will such a tre-
mendous soul lead thee ? If it
take thee out of Stratford, I
shall die.

Will
Shakespeare

Wait ! thou rememberest,

surely, the day we walked by the Avon and I did tell thee of La Pucelle, the man-maid of France, born in the furrow and wedded to the plow and how she heard strange voices and saw forms come back from Heaven and how she for a time won battles and propped a throne.

Hannah Hathaway

Yea, and I did tell thee that I would not greatly love to hear such voices or see such figures, but would for my part keep close to the plow and say prayers for stoneless furrows. I wish thou wert less bold of spirit, Will.

Will Shakespeare

Those who are called to from out the air, those who

are permitted to hear the voices, must listen to their charges or they anger the Gods. Hannah, girl, I hear these voices, I see these figures, or figures like unto them. Day and night, hour after hour, I look on a passing spectacle, an unrolling of scenes that have been acted and I feel that it is for me to whom these strange things are shown to put them into some great and perpetual verse.

Hannah
Hathaway

And these things thou seest, these things thou hearest, are they not all in the Chronicles?

Will
Shakespeare

The fall of a king is indeed chronicled in the histories, but how fell the king? The throne was strong; whence came the wind which over-toppled it? It is this story I shall tell. I see the shadows and eclipses of events, the patient weaving of wicked patterns, the parcellings of purposes, the preparation of vilest instruments; I hear the planning of cunning tongues in secret council, the treacherous engagement of foreign Princes, the eloquent speech of Senates, the building of Trojan horses, the shaking tread of marching hosts, the mighty clash of arms and—then falls the King. I shall enumerate and string the very cords that move the human heart and that move the world. I will give the cause of happened things, the cause, the causes and every several part which by multiplying can itself cause a cause. I will account for each sand grain that goes into the glass to measure the hurrying hour.

Hannah
Hathaway

And will this busy world listen to thee?

Will
Shakespeare

I shall go to London and there make plays. I shall be heard to speak through many mouths. My characters shall stamp and strut in story on the stage. Men shall say "How plain is the falling out of this design. It could not come to other consummation," or "such ambition by travelling such a road must have had end in such abandonment," or "surely such hate must have heated anew the fires of Hell—," or "Love like this must have been born in Heaven and even in this very way is now returned there."

Hannah Hathaway

Ah! Will, thou art spreading a wing that shall bear thee away from me in body and in spirit. I do not like this flight. I shall not have even thy Stratford soul for mine own. Thou wilt no longer love me. Thou wilt see fairer faces, touch softer hands, feel sweeter kisses.

Will Shakespeare

Nay, sweet Ann, a thousand kisses from a thousand mouths shall never borrow the

love I have for thee.   We can-
not contend against my going.
It would be easier to battle
against a King's decree.   It
must be so.   But I shall love
thee absent with an increase of
new affection like hunger brings
to long-stayed appetite.   My
muse shall rehearse its earliest
songs to thee.   My pipe shall
utter into thine imagined ear
each day its choicest notes.
No flower I see shall breathe
other than thy perfume.   The
birds I hear will I think to have
flown from out thy hand and
I will give their wings messaged
burdens to straightway bear to
thee.   And soon the map of
winter will be crossed and with
the first lisping of the spring I

" AND WITH WHAT SOUL LOVEST THOU ME, WILL ? "

	shall see thee once again. Be thou brave and help me keep up to my great designs.
Hannah Hathaway	Will, my Will, do thou here and now swear me a solemn promise never to forget me, never to let me lose thy love?
Will Shakespeare	So will I swear. By what shall I swear?
Hannah Hathaway	Thou believest that the shining stars rule in the affairs of men. I would have thee constant like the stars. Swear then by them—swear by the stars.
Will Shakespeare	Then, that will I do. I do swear by the sun that governs the day, I do swear by the

moon that rules the night, I do swear by the stars that ever have their will of men, never to forget thee, my Hannah Hathaway, never, never, never.

(Curtain falls on scene I.)

SCENE II

SCENE II

(Charlecote forest at night. The trees are elms and willows. A shot is fired in the distance. Soon after enter two foresters, Joseph Carnaby and Euseby Treen.)

Euseby Treen

JOSEPH CARNABY, what was that! Was't a gun?

Joseph Carnaby

It surely was a gun and spake its piece not far from Mickle Meadow. 'Tis there the deer go down at night to drink. Let us keep in the shadow of these elms and willows and we soon shall see.

Euseby Treen

I do not like to pry into shots and noises like unto

these. Nor do I like the forest at night. Two and thirty years, boy and man, have I kept guard by day in these woods but never yet did I meddle with them by night. I would I were at the tavern. The memory of ale is troubling my throat greatly.

Joseph
Carnaby

Let the ale await thy tankard and let thy tankard await thee. There will be a gallant company of tankards for us both if we obey Master Silas Gough and if we arrest Will Shakespeare with his *fragrant dilect*—though for my part if we do find him only with a slain deer I think we shall have done a good night's work.

Euseby Treen

Then do thou arrest the lad and I will seize the deer. If the deer be properly dead I can bear it hence or if his throat be so cut that he be fair on his way to dying I shall end his life. I am a master hand with a dying deer and that thou knowest—and all the parish knows it—but I nearly die with thirst. If I had but what I left in the brown mug at the noon hour!

Joseph Carnaby

Nay, there may be as many as ten lusty villains employed in this robbing gang and they would have of us our lives as quickly as a bird's.

Euseby Treen

I say let the woolstapler's son alone. We can summon

him before the Justice in the light of day on the morrow and I can imagine the killing of the deer, aye, and aver to the same as well as if I did stop to behold it. I cannot see well in the night and already begin to feel ill of the trees. I will run to the tavern, Joseph, and will send the stable lad, a good stout youth and famous with the cudgels. But what hast thou now, what seest thou up there, Joseph ?

Joseph
Carnaby

I did see a star fall from out the heavens straight down to the earth and drop like a ripened nut from off the highest tree.

Euseby
Treen

Then we are lost ! If so be

that a single star be gone from the sky it will be brought home to us, for thou didst see it first in the heavens and then did see it drop and if it be charged to us, we shall die for it. No, no, Joseph, come away, come away to the tavern.

Joseph
Carnaby

We have bound ourselves to do this for Master Silas and we must keep near unto our word.

Euseby
Treen

There is harm in this business and if it be Lucifer that thou didst see drop down out of the sky, it is certain that the Evil One himself is joining in this night's work. Joseph, Joseph, let us say our prayers !

Joseph Carnaby	Thou art the foolishest forester in the three parishes if thou thinkest that the Evil One would mind such as us when there are so many in the world trying to do good and fashioning pious works. He will have big hands to thwart and deal with their plans and will give us never a thought.
Euseby Treen	Aye, man, in truth it is a sweet comfort at a time like this when the devil is seen by our own eyes to be abroad, to think that we have done no great good in our lives to have made him unhappy, nor have we prevented the working of some evil in which perhaps Lucifer had much heart. No,

I feel that thou art right and we have not angered the good Lucifer, the kind Lucifer, the sweet, fair and just Lucifer, the —(Just then Will Shakespeare's voice is heard in the far distance singing.)

Will Shakespeare	The Devil went searching for men and for Priests, He searched through the forests, he searched through the streets, And whenever he gathered a faithless fat soul He plunged it adown to the brim-stony bowl.

Oh ! the Devil was busy
  And his hand it was sore,
But he wriggled his pitch-fork
  And cried for yet more:

"Fattened Priests all in black or good lay-men in buff—"
But when he gets Silas he'll have Devil enough.

Joseph Carnaby	In the name of Heaven, Euseby Treen, get down on

thy knees and let us commend our souls to God. I did not think so fair a night could grow such clouds of brimstone. Thy sweetness toward the Devil hath well nigh lost us our souls to say nothing of our precious bodies. Get down on thy knees, man, down on thy knees.

(Both kneel and mumble prayers to God for mercy and protection ; Euseby being loudest in his exclamations for help from Heaven and of hostility to the Evil One. At this instant Shakespeare appears at one wing with a deer slung across his shoulders in such a manner as to bring the horns of the buck over his own head, and beginning to sing another song—

Will Shakespeare

"The Mermaid, the Mermaid"—

Euseby Treen

(Looking up and seeing the apparition.) Oh! Good Lord, the Devil! Oh! the Devil, my good Lord! Oh Joseph Carnaby, that thou shouldst have made me take back the good words I did speak of the Devil and behind his back. Here is his worshipful face and thou hast ruined my soul, Joseph, else had the Devil, the sweet Devil, not have come to take us. I ever loved thee, Oh! Lucifer, Oh! good Devil—

(Both kneel trembling until Shakespeare comes forward.)

Will Shakespeare	Aha, my brave foresters, what seek ye on your knees? Art laying wiles for birds? Shame on ye for ensnaring the Knight's game in his own forest and in the Lord's own night. Shame on ye I say.
Joseph Carnaby	(As both rise from their knees.) We do know thee well, but before we have further speech of thee we would ask how many men do make thy company?
Will Shakespeare	There would be with me eight more men of my own veritable mien and disposition —an I were a tailor. Being a simple shepherd, I am alone.
Joseph Carnaby	Thou art no shepherd, but

	the son of the woolstapler of Stratford.
Will Shakespeare	Well-a-day, the woolstapler hath the last of the sheep. He hath the skin and he hath the wool and he that hath the last of a thing is the keeper of the thing and a shepherd is the keeper of what distinguisheth a sheep, and ergo, a woolstapler is a keeper of the sheep and therefore is a shepherd.
Joseph Carnaby	(Aside to Euseby Treen.) He is alone, man, and we be two!
Euseby Treen	Truly Joseph, the lad doth prove fairly himself and family to be shepherds. A keeper of sheep and a keeper of deer to

my mind do appear in a sense to be of a brotherhood. Doth it not seem to thee we had best leave him alone ?

Joseph Carnaby

An thou art alone, Will Shakespeare, we do take thee into custody in the Queen's name, and do thou, Euseby Treen, proceed to seize upon him. If thou but layest thy hand upon his shoulder in the Queen's name he shall be the same as in prison and in bonds, aye and peradventure under the rope's noose as well.

Euseby Treen

Do thou stand quiet, good Master Will, and lay down thy gun and do thou fold thine arms, for I am about to arrest by judicial seizure thy carnal body and I am a forester, aye, and a constable of the peace and I am a man of good spirit, afraid of nothing mortal and a very lion when provoked by the villainous and an angry tiger when enraged by the unlawful, so that men do say, "Beware of Euseby Treen, the forester," "It is best to yield at the first charge to Euseby Treen, the constable."

Will Shakespeare

Indeed I do stand in dreadful awe of thee and of thy valiant courage, good Master Constable, but before I yield this poor bit of clay to gyves and chains, thou must show thy warrant. The late King

Henry of blessed memory and the King and Queens of his begetting, have secured to the poor and lowly a goodly chance of Justice. When I do see thy warrant and behold my name writ out in big letters, then shall I know that I am apprehended in the eyes of the law and out of the very teeth of circumstances. Show then thy warrant.

(Joseph Carnaby and Euseby Treen are consulting and the latter is overheard to say "We shall be protected by Master Silas," to which Carnaby replies, "Do not drag in the name of the Priest, we shall do well if we use it not here.")

Joseph Carnaby	We have no warrant nor have we need of warrant. Dost think we carry the Great Seal in our hand and the Queen's vellum commission, a whole yard long, in our coat? We have our staves as authority and thou knowest well we are the Parish Constables.
Will Shakespeare	And of what am I charged?
Joseph Carnaby	With being in unlawful and felonous and murderous possession of a deer from out Charlecote forest.
Will Shakespeare	Then am I innocent, for I have no deer.
Joseph Carnaby	No deer, no deer! then in

the name of the beasts of the field, what is that thing there ?

Will Shakespeare

Do not give utterance to those monster swearings, Joseph Carnaby, do not take in vain—speaking the name of creatures made by thy Creator. Art thou not afraid the heavens will fall on thee ?

Euseby Treen

Aye, Joseph, withdraw thy wicked oath, Joseph, else the other stars, the brothers and sisters and children of Lucifer, will fall on us.

Will Shakespeare

There hast thou a pious example, Joseph. Why dost thou not shape thy words and thy faith to the grave and

	seemly conduct of thy good fellow constable ?
Joseph Carnaby	Thou hast as many words as a dog hath fleas and they do worry and irritate a thousand fold worse—but the point in the law is that thou art in possession of a deer.
Will Shakespeare	The point in the law then is that I am not in possession of a deer. I was in a distant sense in possession of or holding a certain remote and accidental relationship to a carcass, a dead body, a lifeless piece of venison, but not a deer, not a deer, Joseph. A deer is a living thing, that leaps and pants, that nibbles the dew-moistened grass, that drinks the

cooling water from out the water lily cup, that so looks appealingly into the human eyes of the hunter who seeks his life that I do marvel thou canst have the heart, even shamefacedly, to talk of killing and destroying and of shambles and of venison pasty.

Joseph
Carnaby

It is a hanging matter.

Will
Shakespeare

It is not a hanging matter to be in possession of a carcass, or else when thou art dead they shall hang a wooden box full of worms.

Euseby
Treen

Truly, Joseph, thou art in the wrong, for the lad hath already shown he hath no deer but a carcass and I do not think we can hold him in justice of equity. And thou hast irritated him and bullbaited his words until he hath begun to talk of worms, crawling worms, viperous worms, man-eating worms, things which living I never shall learn to abide. He hath reasoned this out well and stoutly to my understanding, Joseph, and I say let him and his worms crawl fast and far away.

Joseph Carnaby

He hath chopped logic into pieces until the face of truth looks like the pustules and pimples on Granny Madden's face. I cannot answer his tongue-thrusts, but words that come out of his throat shall not keep the rope from going around about it.   The deer is before our very eyes!

Will Shakespeare

Whose deer sayest thou this is or was?

Joseph Carnaby

It was one of the herd from out the forest of Charlecote and therefore the sole property and fief and entail and estate of Sir Thomas Lucy, Knight and Esquire and Most Worshipful Justice of the Peace for these Parishes.

Will Shakespeare

Well, this particular and singular entail is well cut off. But knowest thou this especial and individual deer?   Canst thou swear on oath and before the judgment place that this

carcass ever belonged of right
to a deer which in turn did be-
long to Sir Thomas? Hast
thou private notches cut upon
his horns? Are his antlers
marked with the branches of
his ancestral descent? Dost
thou recognize his eyes, his
hair, his nose, his hoofs, his
tail and wilt thou make full
and complete inventory of all
his several parts in thine oath?

Joseph Carnaby

Nay, but Euseby Treen can,
for he doth know every hair on
the hide of every deer in
Charlecote.

Will Shakespeare

As thou knowest every hair
on the head of every *dear* in
Stratford, thou and thy wench-
seeking master, Silas Gough.

But what sayest thou, Euseby Treen, thou fearless guardian?

By my faith, and by my word and by my sacred oath, I am not sure this night of what I do know. What with falling stars and songs to the honor and glory and sanctification of Devils and Mermaids, and wrestling bouts with logic and twisting of words, what with wooden coffins and wriggling, slime-mouthed worms, I do not rightly think I can swear to mine own valor. I would swear to the old brown doe who was big with young, for I did see her drop her male fawn under the crooked elm by the bottom of the meadow.

It was this very day just as noon had grown old by two full hours and I did mark her well. And likewise this buck, I am of a moral surety, was the very one that did horn-thrust at me last rutting season, and I would have sworn to him, too, with a ready tongue until evil doers began to talk of worms and hangings.

Will Shakespeare

And this buck did angrily attack thee ?

Euseby Treen

That he did and murder-ously.

Will Shakespeare

(Aside.) I thank thee, Euse-by Treen, for this avenue out of Charlecote forest.

Joseph Carnaby	Didst thou not put down this buck in the making of thine inventory yesterday to the Knight's clerk ?
Euseby Treen	Aye, that I did and truly too, but yesterday was a day better than this and it had a pleasant and a peaceful night going before it, not like unto this.
Will Shakespeare	And how many deer didst thou report unto the Knight's clerk as his red and entailed deer ?
Euseby Treen	Two and eighty were the number, two and eighty—for I do remember distinctly and openly five "twos" and four

naughts and each naught was set down opposite its own "two" and then there was one "two" which did have no naught with it but which did stand off by itself and good Ephraim Barnett did remark that the mated figures counted up eighty and that the unmarried "two" brought the entire matter up to eighty and two.

Will
Shakespeare

I would I had thy gift of elucidation. It might serve me a good turn in unrolling doubts and in solving problems. But tell me, yesterday the good Knight had two and eighty deer, no more and no less?

Euseby Treen	Aye, and to that I will fill a paper with crosses.
Will Shakespeare	And this dead buck being no longer a deer but only a toothsome carcass would leave his herd short by a single deer, so that there should be but one and eighty, and I am charged with the caused depletion ?
Joseph Carnaby	That is the sum and the figure and the weight and the measure of the matter. The Knight hath only eighty-one deer by reason of thy removing hand, when his book roll will disclose and demand of Euseby Treen two and eighty.
Euseby Treen	Thou hast put it pertly and

smartly, Joseph Carnaby, and the lad stands charged before us two, being two arms as it were of justice, with purloining and felonously abstracting one of eighty and two deer.

.

Will Shakespeare

Thou didst bear witness just now to the big brown doe dropping on the velvet sward beneath the meadow elm this very day a buck fawn, and that I trow hath well supplied the missing figure of one, so that at this very moment, just as at the moment yesterday when the Knight did get his inventoried list, he still owneth, possesseth, holdeth and maintaineth two and eighty deer living and complete in all their parts. Therefore neither can Euseby Treen be charged with permitting the purloining of a single deer nor can I, the gentle, innocent shepherd lad, be justly charged with abstracting one of eighty-two nor any several part thereof. What sayest thou, Euseby Treen?

Euseby Treen

Thou makest thy figures singularly truthful and I ever heard that figures would breed no lies. But surely thou didst steal the deer?

Will Shakespeare

Thou art wrong. What is it to steal?

Euseby Treen

Truly, the best whipped of school-boys knoweth that to

steal is to remove unlawfully the property of another from off his premises.

Will Shakespeare

Then have I not stolen, for on whose premises stand we all three, and on whose premises reposeth the beautiful carcass of yonder deer ?

Euseby Treen

Marry, on the premises of Sir Thomas Lucy, Knight and Justice.

Will Shakespeare

Then have I removed nothing lawfully or unlawfully from off his premises and thy charge is false and fallen to the ground. This carcass which thou pretendest to have seen in my company is still on the premises of Sir Thomas Lucy, Knight and Justice, and I do renounce all acquaintanceship with it. I will have none of it, none of it.

Euseby Treen

Joseph, it doth appear more plainly by figures and by expositions that we cannot hold the lad—but what sayest thou?

Joseph Carnaby

I say, away with him at once to Sir Thomas and listen no more to senseless words.

Will Shakespeare

But if thou art to arrest me what wilt thou do with my companions should I call them to my aid? Wilt thou arrest them likewise? Wilt thou contend against many?

Joseph Carnaby

Thou didst declare that thou hadst no companions.

Will Shakespeare	See now how careless justice is with her memory! Thou didst ask me how many men were of my company and I declared myself to be alone of men— (aside) as indeed I sometimes think I am in any company— but dost thou not know that there are other things in the world beside men? Hast thou never heard of the spirits which haunt these woods and mountains? They are my friends. I have but to call on the Queen of the fairies, on the elves and sprites, on the pixies and gnomes, on Oberon and Puck and thy lives are lost. If I content myself with humbler things, with their lower servants, I shall have ye harried

into a senseless mass. I will
have the clamorous owl
screech into thine ear, Joseph
Carnaby, until it part with
its hearing; the hedge-hog
shall needle thy shanks and
shins until thou art like
some quarrelsome fellow at a
fair; the furry legged spider
shall weave a net, Euseby
Treen, over thy mouth; batty
wings shall cover thine eyes;
spotted snakes shall slime their
enamelled skin upon thee;
blackest beetles shall encom-
pass thee. In truth there are
things within this forest which
belong more to me than to Sir
Thomas.

Joseph
Carnaby

Thou shalt stay where

"I WILL HAVE THE CLAMOROUS OWL SCREECH INTO THINE EAR, JOSEPH CARNABY."

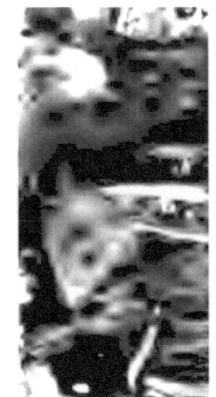

thou art, for us. I want none of thine owls and hedge-hogs !

Euseby Treen

We will away without thee. Keep thou thyself thine obedi-ent bats and snakes !

Joseph Carnaby

Sir Silas, whose errand this is, shall deal with thee.

Will Shakespeare

Oh ! ho ! This business then is the doing of Sir Silas Gough ! Well, then, I will tell thee, I fain would go to him of mine own will. Take thou the carcass and I will follow a docile and contrite prisoner ; not after the customary man-ner of yoked and drooping captives, but still thy prisoner, thy prisoner.

(Exeunt Carnaby and Treen bearing the deer on a stave.)

Will
Shakespeare

These hinds of forests and of men! a little food, a little drink, a little sweating of the brow, a little folding of the hands—and the circumference and contentment of their days are rounded and complete. God forbid me such dull substance! Heaven send me no such consumption of myself. Either I must dwarf my lungs or breathe a larger air. The axe for the woodman, the net for the fisher, but boundless space for him who would write of men. To-day Stratford, to-

"I WILL SWEAR IT ON THE ALTAR OF THY PURE BOSOM, OH
EARTH."

morrow the world ! And for
thee, oh ! Hannah ! This wing
I begin to beat against the air
shall grow in strength until it
bear us both. I will build our
nest on the borders of the sky.
Think not I shall forget thee,
my Hannah ! What was the
oath ? I will swear it again
beneath the benediction of
thine arms, oh ! trees ! I will
swear it on the altar of thy
pure bosom, oh ! earth ! Hear,
oh ! ye winds, that ride the
furthest circuits, hear ye now
my chainêd and solemn vow !
I do swear by the sun that
governs the day, I do swear by
the moon that rules the night,
I do swear by the stars that
ever have their will of men,

never to forget thee, Hannah Hathaway, never, never, never!

(Exit Will Shakespeare and the curtain falls on Scene II.)

SCENE III

SCENE III

(The great hall of Charlecote House. On a large table in the middle of the hall lies the carcass of the deer. At another table, not far from an open window, sits Sir Thomas Lucy, while Ephraim Barnett, the clerk, is arranging papers.)

Sir Thomas Lucy

MASTER Ephraim, what hast thou set down for us this forenoon ? Is it not the trial of the Stratford lad ?

Ephraim Barnett

Aye, your worship, it is the trial of William Shakespeare, a youth of Stratford hard by. I have writ down the lad's name Guilielmus Hasta - Vibrans. The trade of learning should be driven amongst scholars alone and so I may tell your worship that no more warlike name goes up and down in these three parishes, for we do read that amongst the high Germans the name Guilieimus, or Wilhelm, doth signify Helmet of defense and thus this present possessor is armed with a buckler for his head and with a weapon of offense for swift-throwing attack. Men of warlike naming do ever mount upward. Our own countryman and Rome's Pontiff, the fourth Adrian, fetched his name out of Breakspear and your worship mindeth to what high place he did fight his way, albeit he couched with disjointed lance. As

"NAY, HANNAH GIRL, NEVER FEAR FOR ME."

touching our rendering of Hasta-Vibrans, it is indeed true that the older Latinists——

Sir Thomas Lucy

There, that will do, Good Master Ephraim.

(Sir Thomas Lucy turns to papers on his desk. The door opens and William Shakespeare and Hannah Hathaway enter in close conversation.)

Hannah Hathaway

Oh! Will, Will, what a plight thou art in! A thousand snakes have not ensacked the venom Silas Gough hath gathered up for thee. The man will hang thee if cunning and deceit can do it.

Will Shakespeare

Nay, Hannah, thou knowest I believe in the stars and

the stars have not yet written that I shall hang for a bit of tallow and horns and hair.

Hannah Hathaway

Can nothing make thee serious, Will?

Will Shakespeare

After to-day I shall be serious all my life, be my days many or numbered like scattered hairs.

Hannah Hathaway

I shall speak for thee. I shall bear testimony to thy visit to me last night and that thou couldst not have had a purpose of deer killing in thy mind.

Will Shakespeare

I will aver that since Cupid hath armed himself with the deadly bow, I did think it prudent to meet him with a gun.

Hannah Hathaway	Dost thou not fear the Knight, Sir Thomas ?
Will Shakespeare	Why this is the very kindliest Knight that ever blinked at sun. Many times these last few years have I walked by his side and talked with him and yet ever his head hath been bent cloudwards. I verily believe he knows me not from any other lad whose first beard be growing in Stratford. But these walks and talks have turned his gentle soul into a readable book for me. He is like an instrument with few notes, homely and sweet, and this instrument I do fully know and can play upon it a simple air of pardon and forgiveness.

Nay, Hannah girl, never fear for me.

Sir Thomas Lucy

Master Ephraim, hast all ready for the trial ?

Ephraim Barnett

Aye, your worship, all is set and complete as if thou were the greatest Justice of the Oyer and Determiner in the Kingdom. Thou hast thy "dedimus potestatem" from the Lord Chancellor and I have mine office of Clerk of the Peace in the naming from thy good grace as "Custos rotulorum," and while I do set down in the book the speech of truth, nothing thereof shall be frustrate or void—that I can tell your worship. I have

" SEEST THOU THESE GOOD MEN ? "

	commanded in thy name witnesses, that thou mayest examine each "ad perpetuam rei memoriam." I have——
Sir Thomas Lucy	There, that will do, Good Master Ephraim.
	(Silas Gough has entered and spoken to Sir Thomas Lucy who for the first time seems to notice the young couple.)
	Come thou hither, Mistress Hannah, and sit thee here by me. It is not seemly that thou shouldst stand by that scape of grace and village ne'er-do-well, as if to support him in his iniquity.
Hannah Hathaway	Good Sir Thomas, I must

needs stand by him here and now, for I am promised to stand by him everywhere and forever. Of a truth, my Willie hath done no wrong. Thou dost not know him.

Sir Thomas Lucy

Of that, girl, the law, the great and sacred law, must make disposition. Where are the witnesses? Let the witnesses come in and depose concerning the matter.

(Enter Joseph Carnaby and Euseby Treen. Ephraim Barnett the clerk calls each by name and each says to Sir Thomas, "Your Worship.")

Sir Thomas Lucy

William Shakespeare of Stratford - upon - Avon, seest

thou these good men who are deponents against thee ?

Will Shakespeare

(Peering into the faces of the men.) Faith I would indeed rejoice and the neighborhood would have much advantage if I or any honest citizen could see these men good, Your Worship. But Joseph Carnaby and Euseby Treen are henchmen of yonder Silas Gough and therefore they cannot be good nor can they be seen to be good.

Silas Gough

Good in thy teeth, thou virtueless villain.

Will Shakespeare

Aye, good is in my teeth, and behind my teeth, and between my teeth, but it is a fruit thou hast never tasted. It would sadly disconcert thy mouth and overturn the furniture of thy stomach could it but enter those vile caverns.

Sir Thomas Lucy

Nay, thou depraved and ribald youth, thou must bear thyself more becomingly before thy betters. Master Silas did but seek to read thee a timely reproof as his priestly office requireth. He would not have thee understand that good dwelleth in his mouth or proceedeth out thereof, nor indeed would he convey to thy mind that good inhabiteth mine own mouth which is the voice-way of the first magistrate of this shire and properly thy pattern and better, nor yet that good doth or can proceed out of my magisterial and knightly mouth which by mine office is attuned to timely, righteous and true words, but he would fain have thee learn to invite and give glad entertainment to good in thine own teeth, that is to say in thine own mouth and by the office of thine own tongue. (Aside.) This extempore sermon I have read the youth doth not seem to be cut and framed in all its parts as I would have had it. Methinks, somehow, I have hit to one side of the heart of the reproof. But the morning is hot and wanes toward the noon hour, and I am singularly dry of throat.

(To Ephraim Barnett.) Good Master Ephraim, I do pray thee, have me fetched a draught of ale.

(To one of the servants.) Ho there, Abraham, varlet, bear quickly here a well-cooled tankard of ale. Your worship well perceiveth the best office of honest English ale is to nourish England's magistracy. It doth quicken the wit of Judges, it doth unseal the ear of wisdom, it doth open the eye of validity, it doth soften the voice of condemnation, it doth uphold the arm of equity, it doth much enlarge the heart of mercy, it doth speed the feet of errantry, it doth swell the lungs of obligation, it doth counter-strike great mischiefs, it doth devise methods, it doth propagate reasons, it doth reach conclusions, it doth give a passing patrimony to the poor, it doth consecrate cus-toms, it doth minister joys, it doth——

Sir Thomas Lucy

(As the ale is brought him.) There, that will do, Good Master Ephraim, the ale doth very well for me.

Will Shakespeare

Aye, your worship, and every *doth* that Master Ephraim doth brew and every doth of his doth-anatomy doth but add to thy magisterial thirst and to the discomforting of even so unailing a throat as mine own.

Sir Thomas Lucy

Silence, youth, and let me taste the cup of peace. By my Knighthood, I could have furnished good habitation for well nigh a full Kilderkin of this sensible ale. And now, Joseph Carnaby, do thou depose on the charge and with particulars.

Joseph Carnaby

I was returning last night from Hampton in company with Euseby Treen, here, whither we had been on special message to seek tidings of Andrew Haggit who hath absconded. As we passed through the Park we did hear a gun-shot seeming to come from the bottom of Mickle Meadow, and there were loud voices as in mirth and revelry and songs. I plucked Euseby Treen by the doublet and whispered "Euseby, Euseby, there be game stealers abroad, let us lie in the shadow of the elms and willow trees and capture the robbers"——

Euseby Treen

Nay, willows and elm trees were the words.

Will Shakespeare

See, your Worship, what discordances. They cannot agree on their own story. They cannot connive in harmony. They cannot even lie together under the shadow of the same trees.

Silas Gough	The same thing, the same thing in the main.
Sir Thomas Lucy	The terms are much synonymous and thou mayest hang for this crime even were there no willow or elm trees in the forest.
Joseph Carnaby	(To Euseby Treen.) The Knight will hang him out of hand, mark that, Euseby. We may as well step forth and choose the length of hemp.
Will Shakespeare	By less differences have estates been lost, Kings deposed, homes broken and England, our country, filled with homeless, helpless, destitute orphans. I protest against it.

Silas Gough	Protest, indeed. He talketh like a member of the House of Lords. The Lords alone can protest.
Sir Thomas Lucy	The objection doth not appear to me to be momentous and thou mayest have thine ears slit for this charge and no account taken in the law for this discrepancy.
Euseby Treen	(Aside to Joseph.) Get thou the knife, Joseph, for surely the Knight will fringe the lad's saucy ears. He will evermore go about the Parish with ribbons on the sides of his head.
Joseph Carnaby	I would we could slit his tongue. It would greatly

mend his words and his man-
ners.

Nay, Your Worship, thou
must hear me patiently for I
have written more than an
entire year in an Attorney's
office and have read much of
the statutes and the laws and
I do know the sacred rights
which great judges like thee
do guarantee unto humble
Englishmen like me, and I
would therefore protest under
the law, under the law. I
would remind Your Worship
with respect of the heavy fine
laid upon a gentleman magis-
trate of an adjoining county in
the reign of the sixth Edward,
for having committed a poor

man to prison for *"being in possession of a hare,"* it being afterward proven from out the mouths of a cloud of witnesses that the hare was at the very time in the possession of the poor man and not the poor man in the possession of the hare.

Sir Thomas Lucy

(Somewhat moved) I do not at this moment recall the case thou hast cited from the books, but we will go on with the trial and do thou, Joseph Carnaby, be more circumspect with thy sworn testimony.

Joseph Carnaby

We were in the shadow of the—the trees—the trees, some score of furlongs from the robbers——

Sir Thomas Lucy

Thou hast said it already—all save the furlongs—(to Ephraim) hast room for the score of furlongs, worthy Ephraim?

Ephraim Barnett

Aye, Your Worship, and would have were they as many good English miles. I shall write mainly in small rounded letters which though they be like ciphers in form are without distortness in the intent. My quill was plucked by a wart-fingered lad in the full of the moon, less three days, at Candlemas from a gray-black goose and ground one hour from break of day on a blood-red stone from the bed of a month-dried brook. It is a quill which dare cover much parchment and in some hands would outswear a score of witnesses. But your worship well knoweth the honor in which I hold mine office. What saith the proverb: "Anser, Apis, Vitulus, Populosque Regna gubernant," that is to say, Vitulus, the parchment to bear the message; Apis, the wax to hide its meaning from the pry of men and Anser, the goose which doth provide the pen to indite the same, these three do rule——

Sir Thomas Lucy

There, Good Master Ephraim, that will do.

Will Shakespeare

Your Worship will observe the good clerk hath stuck the hide on the little bee in the stead of upon the bigger and stronger calf.

Sir Thomas Lucy

Silence, youth. I know thy skill, Ephraim, and that there be great flights in thine Anser, so that thou leanest not too weightily on the neb.

Will Shakespeare

An', Sir, so hast thy Court ever both interrogator and Anser.

Sir Thomas Lucy

Silence, silence, I say, bold youth, and abide in quiet. (Aside to Silas Gough.) Methinks, Silas, the lad hath caught something of my wit. We may yet break him into a steady drawing beast. The whistle, mayhap, will do more than the whip.

Silas Gough	The whistle will blow away. The whip will leave its good writing up and down the flesh.
Sir Thomas Lucy	Go on, Joseph Carnaby, go on. It doth appear by thy testimony that there were a huge and desperate gang afloat. We have the leader and chief of the robber-band and we shall forthwith—but I must act with prudent speed as becometh an English magistrate. So, do thou proceed, Joseph.
Joseph Carnaby	I said unto Euseby, "Euseby Treen, there seemeth to be at least ten in this crowd of evil-doers——"
Euseby Treen	Twelve, Joseph—twelve—

nay, it *was* ten—thou art right, Joseph, ten was the exact number that thou didst mention. It was twelve I had fixed in mine own imagining—saying unto myself, "Euseby, six of these dreadful robbers must thou capture, while Joseph taketh his own six." But the twelve were in my imaginings.

Will
Shakespeare

Aye, Your Worship, the twelve were in the imagination of Euseby Treen, and the ten in the imagination of Joseph Carnaby, for I do declare that in Charlecote forest last night I was alone and without the company of a human soul.

Sir Thomas
Lucy

(To Ephraim Barnett.) Hast

set down the ten rogues in the
Park, Ephraim?

Ephraim
Barnett

Aye, your worship, an' I do
marvel that nine of them may
yet be in that sacred inclosure.
The fat deer are daily dimin-
ished in England and the God-
less no longer do have regard of
her noble Parks whereof she
once was more blessed than
the whole of Europe besides.
The time was when living deer
raised the stomachs of Gentle-
men with their chase and after-
wards, being made venison,
greatly nourished and soothed
them with their flesh. Great
Parks were there in England
before the Conquest and in the
Book of the Doomsday we do

have report of Parcus Silvestris bestiarum. The first King Henry did encompass with a wall of stone——

Sir Thomas Lucy

There, Good Master Ephraim, that will do. Go on, Joseph, thy testimony convinceth. Shall not a Knight have his own Park free of marauding dogs? Shall not his deer be free to live or come to his table as he may direct? I do tremble to think of what England may be coming to in these latter days. But I am a sworn magistrate.

Silas Gough

Aye, the law is under thy feet.

Will Shakespeare

Oh! Great Spirit of Justice

and of Jurisprudence and of Institutes! The law under the feet of an English subject and of an English magistrate. Oh! that I should have lived—and being yet of tender years—to hear the desperate charge that the law is trampled under foot by one of the uprightest Judges in the Kingdom, a man of probity, a man of extreme judicial learning, a man of God's own divine clemency, a prudent Judge, a wise Judge, and to hear it charged by a mere Priest, an unworthy altar-servant, that this great Judge hath trampled under his foot the Law, the sacred Law! Oh! most worshipful Justice, pray do thou commit me, convict me forthwith, conduct me even this very moment to the gallows—I can no longer live to be in the memory of this vile charge and peradventure of its repetition.——

Silas Gough

Dog of a woolstapler's litter, thou oughtest in truth to be hanged. (To Sir Thomas.) Your Worship knoweth full well that nothing was more distant in intent from my heart and my purpose than to utter disparagement of my Patron and my Master ; but this vile word-player would distract a saint.

Sir Thomas Lucy

Nay, good lad, contain thyself. Thou art sensitive for

respect and consideration and
propriety beyond thy years.
Thou doest well to be in alarm
at any word of disrespect to-
ward the law—and indeed I did
not think it in thee—for on the
law doth stand this ancient
Kingdom, its armaments, its
parliaments, its great Queen's
majesty, its established Church
of God, nay, even its very
Knights and Justices. But, lad,
I wot not Master Silas only did
intend to show that as the rep-
resentative of Justice, I, a mag-
istrate, did rest for authority
upon the law, as one might be
said to stand for a foundation
upon a rock, the rock being
law, but the rock is not hurt
by the standing upon it, nor is

	aught of disrespect shown thereto. But I do like well thy solicitude for the great majesty of the law and, Silas, methinks thou mightest have chosen more fitting metaphors and similitudes.
Will Shakespeare	Now, Silas, may God make thee as humble as thou art made humbled.
Sir Thomas Lucy	Be silent, lad. Go on Joseph, and with speed, for the morning passeth.
Joseph Carnaby	And then we did hear voices singing of a mermaid——
Will Shakespeare	Your Worship well knoweth a mermaid hath not been seen this far up the Avon these twenty years and more.

Joseph Carnaby	Nay, but we did hear distinctly this lad singing of a mermaid.
Euseby Treen	Aye, that we did truly—and I thought I could hear her tail sloshing in the brook.
Sir Thomas Lucy	William, didst thou sing of the water-devil-woman ?
Will Shakespeare	I did sing a song I learned long ago.
Sir Thomas Lucy	I fain would hear it now and incorporate it in the weight of judgment which it grieveth me sore to say seems accumulating much on one side of the scales. Sing the song, lad, that the law may make judgment.

Will Shakespeare

The song as I recall it did go like this:

The sea-maid rode on the Dolphin's back,
Rode thro' the waves on the sea-made track,
    And her tresses were black—
      Alack, so black—
    And her tresses were black, Hey, ho.

The mermaid landed the rocks upon
And deceived a Knight with locks auburn,
    And her tresses turned green—
      I ween—so green—
    And her tresses turned green, Hey, ho.

A white-robed Priest next passed that way,
To her beguilings his soul gave sway,
    And her tresses turned white—
      The sight—so white—
    And her tresses turned white, Hey, ho.

She is seen no more on land or sea,
And Priest and Knight are ever more free,
    From the snare of her hair—
      Tho' fair—the hair—
    From the snare of her hair, Hey, ho !

Sir Thomas Lucy

There is not wanting something of cadent melody in

thy verse, lad, but methinks thou hast not been impartial between the lines, giving to some more words than thou hast bestowed upon others and I ever liked evenness of song. Besides methinks the subject badly chosen. Folks reputed to be of sea nativity had best be left to themselves by us of the land.

Silas Gough

Aye, and what hath such as this rogue to do with white-robed priests and knights of auburn hair. Such villains as he are fit only to fall horizontally before their betters or to hang perpendicularly on the gallows.

Will Shakespeare

Faith, I can play the part of

Priest to a wonder by swinging away to the further comparison-pole of thy figure and conversation. Piety, Priest Silas, is thy business, but thou art left-handed in thy trade because of thy wicked proneness.

Sir Thomas Lucy

Touching Priests, Silas, it seemeth me there should be a certain latitude of allusion permitted poets and writers and perhaps a certain familiarity, since the priest is the medium between salvation and the weaknesses and frivolities of the world. Am I not in the right, Master Ephraim?

Ephraim Barnett

Aye, your worship, very

right—that is to say quite right, or right in a measure, that is in a certain measure or in a certain light, somewhat differing in medium and complexion, or as one might say of a contrary appearance, that is to say wrong, quite wrong; for it doth appear by some proofs read out of the book "De Gestis Herewardi" that priests were in the ancient days of that great honor that Knights did bow down before them, and it is written that they were clothed with great power, so that the holy Abbot of Canterbury in the reign of William Rufus did confer honorable Knightdom upon a gentleman—the Abbot being "in

sacra vesta" and the gentle-
man——

There, that will do, Good
Master Ephraim. But a knight,
albeit his hair should be auburn,
a color methinks not grown of
legitimate English air, is of a
finer and higher kind and it ill
becometh a verse maker to take
aught of liberty with his knight-
hood or his doings.   It tendeth
toward the breeding of dis-
respect and the decay of vener-
ation to draw a knight to de-
struction by the tresses of a
mermaid.   Hast thou forgot
St. George and the Dragon—
and is a Dragon less to be
feared than a sea-woman? I
speak now not as a Knight nor

	yet again as a Christian but as one who observeth the various strengths and forces of dragons and mermaids.
Will Shakespeare	Now is my mind enlarged by this learning and I do thank my good fortune for bringing my slow and feeble intelligence under the bright light of a Knight's gracious mind.
Sir Thomas Lucy	Silas, the lad is teachable. He is a conducible youth and we must not let him hang.
Silas Gough	What ! Would Your Worship let loose on the Parish a stealer of deer, a lover of wenches, a maker of verses ? Will the silver service be safe on mine own church altar ?

Will the coffins of the ancient Lucys be unrifled in their vaults? Will the gold rings remain upon the fingers of the dead? Shall a magistrate turn justice out of the door to force in thereat undeserved clemency? I do greatly fear for the Parish.

Sir Thomas Lucy

Thou art right, Silas, yet it goeth against my grain to hang the lad. Let us hear more of the witnesses. Go on, Joseph Carnaby, what then passed after the song?

Joseph Carnaby

The matter then was sharp and short. I did command Euseby Treen to fasten on the robbing, deer-stealing villain and we brought him off to the Hall.

Sir Thomas Lucy

The Parish is secure with such brave and worthy constables. I do commend and marvel at thy courage, for neither art thou nor Euseby youthwards of the side of cudgels and sharp stick-play and the robber did have his gun, tho' it appeareth from thy testimony it had already belched itself empty. Did the fellow attempt to dishonestly suborn thee, Joseph?

Joseph Carnaby

Nay, it would take many a shilling to suborn one such as me, and he had never a piece in pocket or till.

Euseby Treen	(Aside to Joseph.) Joseph, it had been wiser, now I remember the lad's father hath money, had we given him more opportunity to attempt suborning. (Aloud to Sir Thomas.) No, Your Worship, there was no time for suborning either of us, no good opportunity — (becomes silent as Joseph plucks his doublet).
Sir Thomas Lucy	Thou art faithful constables and honest men. What sayest thou, Will Shakespeare, to the charge ?
Will Shakespeare	Your Worship must know that I do now and again walk about under the stars to catch something of fancy and phan-

tasy, being given to poetry and such writing——

Sir Thomas Lucy

Aye, but it is not well to concern thyself with stars and such things. Familiarity doth breed disrespect. I did hear of a man once who thought so little of the noon-day sun that he would gaze up into its very face and forthwith set to sneezing in seeming rebellious disregard of its greatness and power. But, go on, lad, go on.

Will Shakespeare

I was walking through the forest contemplating the great goodness of God in giving the ownership of those lordly trees to so worthy a Knight, when suddenly the bushes gave way and an angry, snorting buck-deer made as if to run me through with his spikes. I drew back and in my fright the gun did discharge and the deer lay dead at my feet. Being dead, it was no longer a deer, but venison and being venison I was no longer in great dread thereof. I thought what a strange pity to leave it to rot when Master Silas might have a chance to smell it basting and to move his godless teeth through its fattened ribs. So I was fetching it out of the forest to bear it to Charlecote House when these two fellows were sent by fortune to relieve my shoulders of the heavy and unusual burden.

"ENACTING SCENES AND PLAYS ON THE GREEN-SWARD BY THE
AVON"—

... the story ... Brook-
side Castle ... it ... run me
through ... his spear ... I
have back ... it ... from the
... fall discharge ... the deer
... dats in my feet. Being
... it still no matter a deer
... venison ... being venison
I was no longer in great dread
thereof. I thought what a
... to leave it ... not
... whether one might have
... to smell ... tasting and
... now his godless ...
though as ... ribs. So
I was ... it out of the
... to bear it to Charlecote
... when these two fellows
... had by fortune to relieve
me ... of the heavy and
... burden.

Sir Thomas Lucy	A man must ever protect his life against a wild and dangerous beast, but how camest by the gun ?
Will Shakespeare	It hath long been in the air of report that Charlecote forest had a few bucks of ferocious inclining, and only the other day this very deer did attack Euseby Treen and but for his courage had had his life of him.
Euseby Treen	Aye, Your Worship, the lad speaks truth of that deer, and but for my strength and honest cudgeling I had not been here this day to do my duty as a constable. The deer was much given to raging, and I can tell your worship.

Will Shakespeare	(Aside to Euseby Treen.) I will suborn thee finely for that supporting testimony some day, good Euseby.
	(Silas Gough in the meantime has been in secret conversation with Sir Thomas, evidently urging some summary punishment on Will Shakespeare.)
Sir Thomas Lucy	Youth, thou hath made some strong explanation of the death of the deer and thy conversation hath shown that thou art a lad not without parts and with a heart movable by the heavier storms of grace. Thy contemplative mood of mind when in the

forest hath not a little turned
my heart toward thee. But
Silas Gough our spiritual guide
and adviser hath cleared to us
the grave enormity of thy rude
trespassing in the Park, thereby
beyond doubt provoking in the
first instance the deer to his
threatening movement, and the
good chaplain hath likewise
brought to our notice thy con-
stant conduct these last sum-
mers in enacting scenes and
plays on the green-sward by
the Avon, and in drawing into
thy wanton company half the
youth in the neighborhood,
imitating Kings, Queens and
Princes, Fairies, Elfs and Sprites,
Cardinals, Knights and Min-
isters, strange men from

France, Venice and Mantua, and even as the story goes, enacting the dusky Moors, with loud mouthings, bold phrases, and with such a shaking of arms, heads and limbs that other villagers have thought the Stratford town delivered over to the Evil One.

Silas Gough

The knave hath no conscience. He hath no knowledge. No decency or humility of youth can find its way down the six appearing hairs of his beard. He hath as much acquaintance with heaven as he hath with a throne or a palace. Dost thou think, thou common player of interludes, that thou and thy crew can

enact the part of Kings and
Queens and go unpunished of
the law? Wouldst thou dare
lay the face or image of a King
or Queen upon a coin of the
realm, and yet thou dost
recklessly counterfeit the entire
person of a Prince. The im-
pression of an Emperor's face
on a farthing is felonous and
rope-worthy. Yet thou and
thy vile actors would imitate
his body and voice, wear his
crown and mantle, strut across
the sward with his majestic
step, and pretend to be royal
and glorious. Out upon thee!
Canst thy shallow brain and
weak conception drink in the
language of Kings? Thinkest
thou that King calleth King,

like thine ignorant players, filch-
er and fibber, whirlagig and
nincompoop. This familiarity
is for the cheese-eating, beer-
drinking guzzlers on the tavern
bench. Instead of this, the
horn blows, the drum beats,
and a thousand fellows like
thee are thrown into death,
and when the Kings have
cleared the land of such scuff,
they render God thanks.
Touch not such high and for-
bidden fruit. When I think of
thy rude boldness I would
have thee wince—thou who
art but the parings of a quince.

Will
Shakespeare

Oh, Your Worship, I pray
thee thank Master Silas in my
unworthy name for these

	words of *wince* and *quince.* Their marriage hath given my memory a jog it hath wanted for this week or more.
Silas Gough	How now, rascal, on what hath thy viperous fangs fastened. I did but say that Kings and Queens were too high and unattainable a fruit for thee to touch who art but as the parings of a quince, a sort of fruit I take to be the meanest ever borne by tree or bush.
Will Shakespeare	Your Worship, it is but a week last Sunday that being in Oxford on my father's business, I sought opportunity to refresh my soul by the rich and

precious sermons which there
fall on scholars. It came to
pass that after a heavy and
saving sermon on the way from
the church the preacher caught
up to me—I having been started
on my way earlier than he, but
stopping now and then to
gauge the instructive points to
the parent text—and the good
man did speak to me and did
deign even to converse with
so humble a hearer. We did
talk of poetry and the large
fields of fruits and flowers open
to the poets, when the Doctor
said unto me, "Lad, not thirty
miles from this very spot there
dwelleth in Knightly retire-
ment the greatest poet of Eng-
land, one who turning aside

from the flowers and fruits which have been gathered by poets old and young and in all times and under all skies, was in truth the first to handle the humble quince." He did then repeat the lines beginning—

" Chloe, I would not have thee wince,
That I unto thee send a quince."

Thereupon I was constrained by my pride to tell him that I lived within three measured miles of the hand that penned those noble lines.

Sir Thomas Lucy

Aye, aye, sensible youth, I did write those verses. Those were the days when I had sweet dreams and insights into the garden of poetry, but alas,

I pursued the muses no great ways.

Will Shakespeare

To the regret of scholars, said Dr. Underhill.

Sir Thomas Lucy

Good lad, didst say Dr. Underhill? Was it with that great man thou didst walk and talk? The learnedest clerk in England?

Will Shakespeare

Even he, and methinks I did walk an inch or two taller remembering that I could pass near to and perhaps see the very fields and forests belonging to this Knightly poet.

Sir Thomas Lucy

William, thou shalt have free passage throughout Charlecote forest and into Charlecote

House. Take heed, Joseph Carnaby, and thou Euseby Treen, this wise and comely youth is to go and come un-questioned by such as ye.

Will Shakespeare

I thank your Worship. Dr. Underhill will be glad to know of this, for he bade me inquire of thee and know if ever the muse moved thee now.

Sir Thomas Lucy

Nay, Will, this knee is a bit stiff to mount Pegasus. But I will give thee copies rounded out in the plain hand of good Ephraim Barnett here, of some of my more polished verses. I do recall another set of verses made from almost as humble fruit, albeit a fruit of the water, and which did make no small stir I am told.   It opened in its first running much like this—

> The Lucy is the finest fish
> That ever lay on garnished dish ;
> Sweeter far than tench or mullet,
> Sea-bred food for Knightly gullet,
> No other Arms or honor choose ye
> Who hath the bone or flesh of Lucy.

(Here Will Shakespeare is shaken with laughter and unable to contain himself.)

Sir Thomas Lucy

I do methink me, Willie, that if thou hearest much more of my poetry and my successes, Dr. Underhill himself could not drag thee away from my skirt.

Will Shakespeare

I would I had a bone from

	the back of that Lucy, Ha! Ha!!
Sir Thomas Lucy	Sweet Will, it is said that the Queen's highness when she did hear these verses said unto her courtiers to the sore travail of some who thought upon themselves as poets— "We need not envy our young cousin of Scotland his thistles, having ourselves such a pike-handling poet by the banks of the loyal Avon."
Silas Gough	The lad may hang without me, for I am called by the voice of my stomach to a delayed dinner.
Will Shakespeare	Your Worship knoweth that

it is better nine other drones like unto Silas be fed unworthily than that one faithful worker shall go famished.

Sir Thomas Lucy

There, sweet Willie, thou must remember Silas is more in years than thou and——

Will Shakespeare

Aye, your worship, but I sorrow that he will not grow wise or good with his years. A minnow by long living will not grow into a whale.

Silas Gough

I plainly see this rope-destined youth can twist and turn other things besides villainous words and irreverent phrases. But I must tell your worship—

" NEVER TO FORGET THEE, MY HANNAH HATHAWAY, **NEVER,**
NEVER, NEVER ! "

(He speaks long and eagerly into the ear of Sir Thomas.)

Sir Thomas Lucy

But, Silas, the youth is reasonable and hath a good mind and will readily consent to thy demand. Boy, Master Silas Gough will be content if thou wilt promise——

Silas Gough

Nay, he must swear, he must make oath !

Sir Thomas Lucy

Well, well, if thou wilt have it so. Good Willie, thou must swear to no longer think upon Hannah Hathaway, here. As Priest and Parish Counsellor and spiritual guardian, I feel that what Master Silas asks of thee is right and seemly. Do thou then take this oath.　Wilt thou ?

Will
Shakespeare

　Oh! that will I, a solemn oath, a trysting oath.　I have already registered an oath of inclination.　Let me register one of compulsion.　Let me quickly take the oath.

Sir Thomas
Lucy

　Good Master Ephraim, give the lad the bound scriptures.

Silas Gough

　Swear thou then to forget Hannah Hathaway and never more go near to Shottery or enter into her mother's cottage.　Swear, swear it.

Hannah
Hathaway

　(With her head in her hands.)　Oh! Will, Will——

Will Shakespeare	Here, then, I do swear—I do swear by the sun that governs the day, I do swear by the moon that rules the night, I do swear by the stars that ever have their will of men, never to forget thee my Hannah Hathaway, never, never, never. (As he says this he throws down the scriptures, jumps through the open window and disappears. Curtain falls and scene ends.) FINIS